W9-BUW-327

This learning tool brought to you by

GSK
Science
in the
Summer™

In partnership with the
Franklin Institute Science Museum

THE
FRANKLIN
INSTITUTE

gsk
do more
feel better
live longer

WITHDRAWN
WITHDRAWN
WITHDR

QWARANTINY

Sports Illustrated KID$

THE SCIENCE OF
HOCKEY

THE TOP 10 WAYS SCIENCE AFFECTS THE GAME

by Matt Chandler

Consultant:
Harold Pratt
President of Educational Consultants
Littleton, Colorado

CAPSTONE PRESS
a capstone imprint

Sports Illustrated KIDS Top 10 Science is published by Capstone Press,
1710 Roe Crest Drive, North Mankato, Minnesota 56003
www.mycapstone.com

Copyright © 2016 by Capstone Press, a Capstone imprint. All rights reserved.
No part of this publication may be reproduced in whole or in part, or stored in a
retrieval system, or transmitted in any form or by any means, electronic, mechanical,
photocopying, recording, or otherwise, without written permission of the publisher.

Sports Illustrated Kids is a trademark of Time Inc. Used with permission.

Editorial Credits

Adrian Vigliano, editor; Sarah Bennett, designer; Eric Gohl, media researcher;
Lori Blackwell, production specialist

Photo Credits

Dreamstime: Jerry Coli, 11 (bottom); Newscom: Icon SMI/Bill Streicher, 10;
Shutterstock: Grushin, 8, stockphoto-graf, 1, 21 (right); Sports Illustrated: Damian
Strohmeyer, 16-17, 18, David E. Klutho, cover, 2, 6, 9, 14-15, 20-21, 22, 23, 27, 29,
Robert Beck, 13, Simon Bruty, 11 (top), Tony Triolo, 4-5

Design Elements: Shutterstock

Library of Congress Cataloging-in-Publication Data

Names: Chandler, Matt, author.
Title: The science of hockey : the top ten ways science affects the game / by
Matt Chandler.
Other titles: Top 10 Science. | Sports Illustrated kids (Capstone Press)
Description: North Mankato, Minnesota : Capstone Press, a Capstone imprint, [2016] |
Series: Top 10 Science | Series: Sports Illustrated kids | Includes bibliographical
references and index. | Audience: 8-10. | Audience: 4 to 6.
Identifiers: LCCN 2015035090 |
ISBN 9781491482216 (library binding)
ISBN 9781491486016 (pbk.)
ISBN 9781491486054 (ebook pdf)
Subjects: LCSH: Hockey–Juvenile literature. | Sports sciences–Juvenile literature
Classification: LCC GV847.25 .C43 2016 | DDC 796.962–dc23
LC record available at http://lccn.loc.gov/2015035090

Printed in the United States of America, in North Mankato, Minnesota.

ELKINS PARK FREE LIBRARY
563 CH   009221CGS16
ELKINS PARK, PA 19027-2445

Table of Contents

Wayne Gretzky is considered by many to be the greatest hockey player who ever lived. But it took more than speed, power, and natural skills. Gretzky had science behind him. The same is true for today's superstars. From Jonathan Toews, to P.K. Subban, to Sidney Crosby, the game of hockey is built on science. Every check, shot, and goal is driven by scientific principles and the top players understand that.

Why can some players skate faster than others? What makes a slap shot whistle through the air at 100 miles (160 kilometers) per hour? How can a small player deliver a bone-crushing check to a much larger player? Get ready to find the answers as we explore the science behind the game of hockey!

▲ Wayne Gretzky

▲ Daniel Sedin

Skating Success

Vancouver Canucks forward Daniel Sedin makes racing down the ice and chasing a puck into the corner look effortless. But how can Sedin move so fast on ice? As a skater moves over the ice, a very thin watery film on the ice surface reduces friction. Scientists know that the pressure of a skater pushing down on the ice causes a tiny amount of melting. At the same time, the **friction** of the skater's blades moving over the ice creates a similar effect.

When Sedin races down the ice, he is skating on vibrating **molecules**. As he moves, the ice and water molecules are shifted by his blades moving back and forth incredibly fast. The pressure and friction of the skate blades increase the speed of fast-moving ice molecules. This forms the slippery surface that allows Sedin to move at top speed.

friction ➠ a force produced when two objects rub against each other

molecule ➠ the atoms making up the smallest unit of a substance; H_2O is a molecule of water

Puck Control

Future Hall-of-Famer Jaromir Jagr is considered one of the best stickhandlers of all time. Hockey players know that stickhandling is a skill perfected through thousands of hours of practice. But being a great stickhandler begins between your ears.

AN ASSIST FOR YOUR STICK

Did you ever wonder how players control a hard pass while skating at full speed? High-speed stickhandling is a difficult task. But players are able to do it better because of how they **modify** their hockey sticks.

A player creates a curve in his or her blade based on position and style of play. For example, a deeper curve acts like a pocket and helps catch the puck. This curve makes wrist shot and forehand control easier and allows the player to put more lift on the puck. But a deep curve also makes backhand and slap shot control more difficult.

Each player wraps a layer of tape over his or her blade before each game. The tape helps with puck control by absorbing the impact of the puck. A frozen puck hitting a smooth blade would be more likely to bounce off. But the rough tape surface softens the impact helps the player stay in control.

modify ➡ to change in some way

8

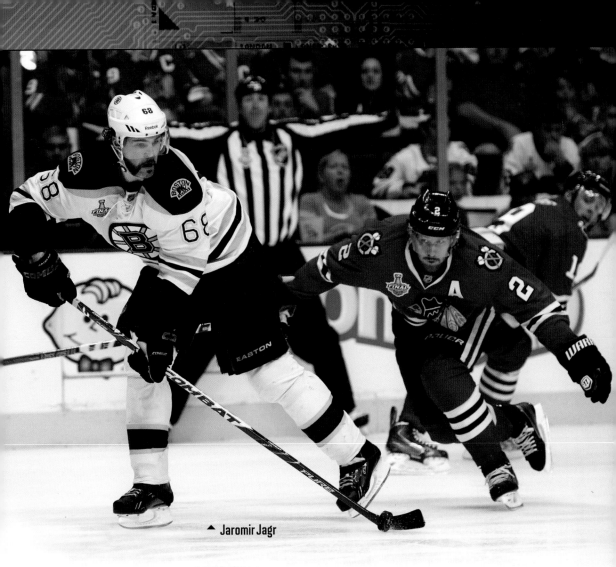
▲ Jaromir Jagr

When Jagr moves up the ice, he has plenty to think about. He needs to know where his teammates and opponents are on the ice. He needs to anticipate the moves of both, all while controlling the puck effectively. Human brains use a part called the temporal lobe to process motion. Some researchers have found that elite athletes can process more information at once than other people. Processing all of this data takes brain capacity. If Jagr can process it twice as fast as another player, he may be able to gain an advantage. An edge in speed and reaction time can be the difference between being an average stickhandler and an elite one.

All About the Ice

Did you know that the ice in an NHL rink is only about one inch (2.5 centimeters) thick? As ice gets thicker, it takes the more energy to keep it frozen. Thicker ice sheets are also more likely to have a soft skating surface, which would slow down players and pucks. But thin ice isn't the only thing that helps NHL players move their fastest.

As Pittsburgh Penguins center Sidney Crosby streaks across the rink, the size and shape of his skate blades reduce friction between his blades and the ice. The more a blade touches the ice, the more friction it creates. To reduce friction as much as possible, skate blades are made very thin. A hockey skate blade is also designed with a curve that leaves two smaller edges touching the ice.

But the goal isn't always to reduce friction. As Crosby finishes his race across the rink, he speeds into the corner after the puck. Suddenly he turns his skates sideways, spraying a shower of ice toward the boards and coming to quick stop. This move allows Crosby to use the friction between his blades and the ice in a different way. By turning his skates against the direction of his movement, the blades cut into the ice. This creates enough friction to stop his forward motion.

◄ Turning the skates sideways and stopping in a spray of ice is a basic skill called the "hockey stop."

◀ **Sidney Crosby**

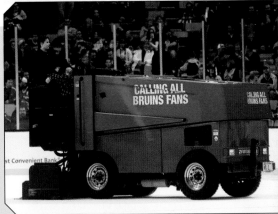

THE ZAMBONI

When the period ends, and the players exit the ice, a Zamboni drives onto the rink and cruises along the ice. While it may look like the machine is just making the used ice shiny again, there is actually more to the process.

Before releasing fresh water onto the ice, the Zamboni shaves off a thin layer of ice to smooth out any rough spots. Then, it applies fresh water, which quickly freezes and gets smoothed over by the machine.

One of the most important parts of the process is the purity of the water. All tap water has dissolved solids in it. Even a small amount of dissolved material can keep water from freezing as fast as is needed for an NHL rink. So before water hits the ice, it is run through a purification machine in the Zamboni. This purified water creates the perfect sheet of NHL ice!

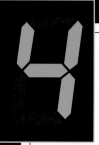

Bone-crushing Physics

Bruising Boards

The tough, physical play in hockey is one of the most exciting parts of the game. Some players are collision experts, checking unlucky opponents into the boards to take control of the puck. Better checking can give a team a big advantage over the opposition. The power of a check depends very much on physics.

If San Jose Sharks defender Brent Burns lines up an opponent for a check, it is usually a big one. But a hit delivered in the corner against the boards is much different than a mid-ice collision. When Burns drives an opponent into the boards, the glass shakes and the noise can be incredibly loud. But that doesn't mean it was the biggest hit of the game.

During a check, **kinetic energy** is transferred from Burns' body to his opponent's body. But if a player is checked into the boards and glass, the barriers absorb some of the hit's energy. The boards of a hockey rink are designed to absorb energy by bending slightly when a player crashes into them. This can mean that the overall effect of a check into the boards creates less movement than one delivered on open ice.

kinetic energy ⟹ the energy of a moving object

▲ Brent Burns hits his opponent with a hard check against the boards.

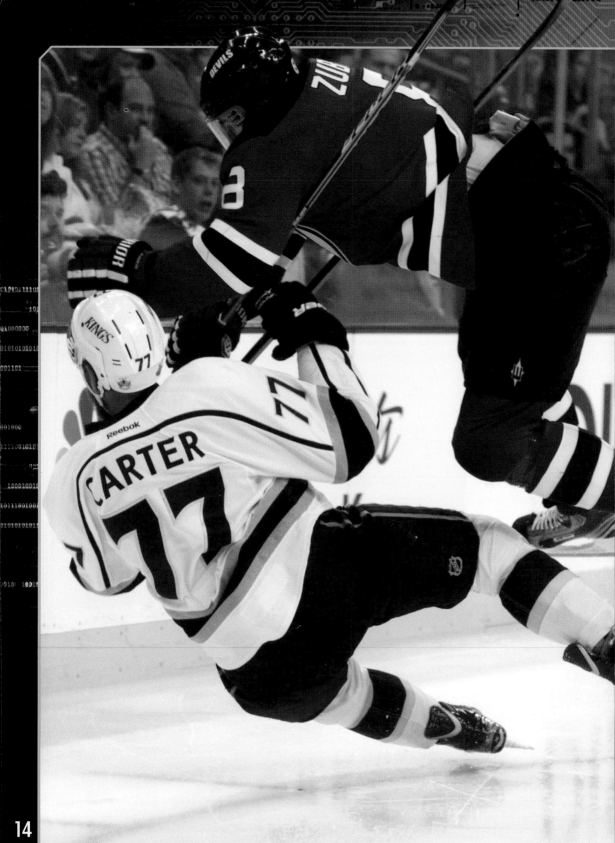

Open-ice Collisions

English physicist Sir Isaac Newton is best known for his three laws of motion. These laws explain how forces affect objects. Newton's first law says that objects at rest stay at rest, and objects in motion stay in motion, unless an outside force acts on them. For example, a hockey player can glide smoothly across the ice until an outside force, such as an opponent's check, interrupts him.

A good check requires a lot of force. The force in a check is produced by the mass of the players and their **velocity** at impact. The bigger a player is and the faster his speed, the more force is used. If one player skates at top speed and delivers an open-ice check to a player skating toward him, a very powerful impact results. Most open-ice hits involve more force than checks into the boards, because both players are likely moving at greater velocities.

velocity ➡ a measurement of both the speed and direction an object is moving

The Perfect Pass

As Washington Capitals winger Alex Ovechkin speeds down the ice, he fires a pass and hits a teammate in stride with a perfect pass. This takes tremendous skill, but players also use science to their advantage.

There are many factors that go into making a great pass. Rough spots on the ice can slow down a puck, as can "snow" that has built up from skates chipping away at the ice surface. Players try to overcome these problems by passing the puck very hard. A hard pass tends to be more accurate and overcomes friction. A typical pass of 60 feet (18.3 meters) takes an average time of one second to reach a teammate's stick.

Newton's third law of motion says that for each action, there is an equal and opposite reaction. We can see this law at work when Ovechkin bounces a puck off the boards. Ovechkin knows the puck will bounce off the boards with an equal and opposite reaction to how he shot it. This ability to predict how the puck will behave when in motion is important. It allows Ovechkin to use the boards as a weapon to pass the puck to a teammate or even back to himself.

▲ Alex Ovechkin

6 The Perfect Shot

Flex and Velocity

Scoring is incredibly difficult. The nets are small and players dive in front of shots, trying to block them before they even reach the goalie. This puts more pressure on each player to develop the best shot possible.

In 2012, Boston Bruins defender Zdeno Chara set the record for fastest slap shot. His shot was clocked at 108.8 miles (175 km) per hour. What is even more amazing is that during a slap shot, the puck only touches Chara's stick for a fraction of a second. In that time, he is able to generate more than 100 pounds (45 kilograms) of force on the puck.

The key to a powerful slap shot comes before Chara's stick connects with the puck. First Chara winds up and brings the blade down to hit the ice well behind the puck. The stick flexes when it hits the ice, and that bowing is what generates the power. Once Chara's blade connects with the puck, the flex in the stick acts like a slingshot and snaps the puck forward, adding extra velocity to his shot.

◀ At six feet, nine inches (2 m) tall and weighing in at 255 pounds (116 kg), Zdeno Chara intimidates opponents with his size as well as his powerful shot.

Rebound Reactions

The rebound shot is another hockey move that shows Newton's third law of motion at work. If Chicago Blackhawks center Jonathan Toews snaps a wrist shot at the other team's goalie, he isn't always trying to score. He may be setting up a teammate in front of the net. Toews knows that the puck will have an equal and opposite reaction when it strikes the goalie's pads. Combining that knowledge with the right aim and timing, Toews can try to bounce the puck off the goalie and toward a waiting teammate. This gives the teammate a chance to blast the puck past an off-balance goalie.

Jonathan Toews (far left) is an expert at setting up goal opportunities for his teammates.

SIX OUNCES OF RUBBER

Perfect passes and shots require a predictable puck. Pucks are made of rubber, an extremely bouncy material. Luckily for hockey players, pucks go through a process called vulcanization. Vulcanization is a way of treating rubber to make it hard, durable, and less bouncy. Each puck is vulcanized to insure it can survive the frozen ice and high-speed slap shots of a game.

To cut down on puck bounciness even more, the NHL freezes every puck before the game and between periods. Cold pucks also slide across the ice better than a warmer puck would.

The side of the puck is imprinted with a special grooved pattern. This texture creates friction when a player's stick touches the puck. This added friction makes a puck easier to handle. The grooves also help shot accuracy by giving shooters better control over spin they put on a puck.

Angling to Protect the Net

When New York Rangers goalie Henrik Lundqvist sees an opponent streaking toward him, he knows that the player with the puck is not his only problem. The first shot may be an attempt to create a rebound for a teammate to set up a goal. Lundqvist knows that controlling rebounds is just as important as stopping shots. And the best way to control rebounds is to understand the science of angles.

When a puck hits Lundqvist, it will bounce back with an equal and opposite reaction. A strong goaltender rarely leaves a rebound in front of the net. By judging the angle at which the puck is coming toward him, Lundqvist can angle his pad or stick to deflect the puck in another direction, away from his opponents. If there are too many opponents surrounding him, Lundqvist may try to use a pad, glove, or stick to stop the shot rather than angling it away. If he can absorb the puck's energy and stop its forward motion, he can fall onto the ice, cover the puck, and safely stop the play.

◀ Henrik Lundqvist is one of the most dominant goalies in the NHL.

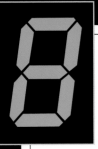

Equipped for Success

Watch any old-time hockey highlight film and you'll see just how far goaltender equipment has come.

Today, most players use hockey sticks made of **composite** materials. But did you know most goaltenders still prefer to use wooden sticks? When a puck smashes into a composite stick, it sends strong vibrations up the stick and those vibrations can sting the goalie's hand. A wooden stick reacts much differently. Wood absorbs more energy than composite materials, so a wooden stick transfers less energy to a goaltender's hand.

For decades, goaltenders didn't wear any protection on their heads. Today, the goalie mask is equal parts safety and fashion statement. But how does a modern goalie mask protect the player from the impact of a high-speed frozen puck? When a puck flies toward the goal at 100 miles (160 km) per hour, it is full of energy. Like all objects in motion, the puck's energy is going to have to go somewhere eventually. If a puck hits a goalie's mask, the puck's energy is transferred into the mask. Like other types of safety equipment, the mask is designed to distribute impact energy over a large area. This doesn't mean a direct hit is painless, but it helps reduce the chance of injuries.

composite ⟹ made of different parts or elements

▲ Nashville Predators goalie Pekka Rinne trusts his protective equipment so he can focus on defending his net.

The Science of the Save

Imagine looking up from the goal and seeing Winnipeg Jets defender Tyler Myers bearing down on you. At six feet, eight inches (2 m) tall and weighing more than 219 pounds (99 kg), Myers is one of the biggest players in the NHL. But though Myers looks intimidating, you can't focus on him if you want to make a save. Researchers have found that the best goalies focus their eyes on the puck and the shooter's stick for a full second before the shot. That second of focus gives goalies a much greater chance of making a save.

There is another crucial element to making the save. When Los Angeles Kings goalie Jonathan Quick sees a shooter approaching, he moves out from the net. If he simply stood in front of the goal, Quick could block around 60 percent of the net.

But if he comes out toward the puck, he reduces the amount of net the shooter can see.

Jonathan Quick tries to position himself so shooters can see as little of the net as possible.

Reaction Time

Measuring the time a hockey player has to react to a shot is easy. The distance from the shooter to the goal divided by the speed of the shot will tell you how long a goalie has to react. It is usually less than one second. The same formula works for measuring reaction time for a defender trying to block a shot or an offensive player receiving a pass.

Players know how quickly games move and how little time they have to react. The closer a shooter is, the less time a defender has to react. Top players, such as Montreal Canadiens defender P.K. Subban, seem to know where a shot or pass is going before it even leaves an opponent's stick. An athlete like Subban has learned to rely on a mixture of **reflexes** and skills developed through practice to get into the proper position.

reflex ⟹ an action that happens without a person's control or effort

It takes the average human less than a second—between 180 and 200 milliseconds—to react to something he or she sees. Researchers have found that, on average, top athletes don't have unusually quick reaction times. A player like Subban has spent a huge amount of time practicing and playing his position. Over time, Subban's brain has built up a database of hockey knowledge that helps him to anticipate where the puck is moving. In the heat of a game, these skills work together with Subban's reflexes, making his reaction time look impossibly fast.

◀ P.K. Subban

GLOSSARY

composite (kuhm-PAH-zuht) ⇢ made of different parts or elements

friction (FRIK-shuhn) ⇢ a force produced when two objects rub against each other

kinetic energy (ki-NET-ik EN-ur-jee) ⇢ the energy of a moving object

modify (MOD-uh-fahy) ⇢ to change in some way

molecule (MOL-uh-kyool) ⇢ the atoms making up the smallest unit of a substance; H_2O is a molecule of water.

reflex (REE-fleks) ⇢ an action that happens without a person's control or effort

velocity (vuh-LOSS-uh-tee) ⇢ a measurement of both the speed and direction an object is moving

READ MORE

Hoena, Blake. *The Science of Hockey with Max Axiom, Super Scientist.* North Mankato, Minn.: Capstone Press, 2016.

Labrecque, Ellen. *The Science of a Slap Shot.* Ann Arbor, Mich.: Cherry Lake Publishing, 2016.

Nagelhout, Ryan. *The Science of Hockey.* New York: PowerKids Press, 2016.

INTERNET SITES

FactHound offers a safe, fun way to find Internet sites related to this book. All of the sites on FactHound have been researched by our staff.

Here's all you do:

Visit *www.facthound.com*

Type in this code: 9781491482216

Check out projects, games and lots more at
www.capstonekids.com

INDEX